D0569672

Mysterious Encounters

ESP

by Kevin Hile

KIDHAVEN PRESS
A part of Gale, Cengage Learning

GALE
CENGAGE Learning™

Detroit • New York • San Francisco • New Haven, Conn • Waterville, Maine • London

LIBRARY OF CONGRESS CATALOGING-IN-PUBLICATION DATA

Hile, Kevin.
  ESP / by Kevin Hile.
    p. cm. — (Mysterious encounters)
  Includes bibliographical references and index.
  ISBN 978-0-7377-4084-4 (hardcover)
  1. Extrasensory perception. I. Title.
  BF1321.H54 2009
  133.8—dc22

                                                                2008045122

KidHaven Press
27500 Drake Rd.
Farmington Hills, MI 48331

ISBN-13: 978-0-7377-4084-4
ISBN-10: 0-7377-4084-1

Printed in the United States of America
2 3 4 5 6 7 13 12 11 10 09

Contents

Chapter 1

The Sixth Sense

A man gets a vision of a series of numbers running through his mind. He decides to play those numbers in a lottery, and he wins!

Police hire a woman to help investigate a missing person case. At the scene of the crime, she tells detectives she has a sense of being cold and wet and that her head hurts. Later police find the body of the female victim floating in a nearby pond. The victim was hit in the head with a hammer.

A man claiming not to be a magician waves his hand near a silver spoon. It bends without him touching it.

These are all examples of extrasensory perception, or ESP. The ordinary human senses are sight, hearing, smell, taste, and touch. ESP, however, goes beyond these regular senses and into a level of perception that some call **paranormal**—events or experiences that go beyond what is considered normal.

Many people do not believe ESP exists. But a Gallup poll conducted in 2005 showed that 41 percent of Americans *do* believe in it.[1] People who are said to have the ability of ESP are often called **psychics**.

Types of ESP

ESP is a broad term that includes several types of sensory experiences. Each form of ESP has its own name.

Precognition is that funny feeling some people get that tells them something is going to happen before it does. Retrocognition is receiving a vision

Telekinesis is the ability to affect objects without touching them, such as bending a spoon using only the mind.

or other information about a past event that the person did not directly experience in his or her life. For example, someone with retrocognition might have a vision of another person's past experience when standing near that other person or when holding something that belongs to that person.

Clairvoyance (which means "clear seeing") is the ability to see things and events that are at a different location and that exist or are happening at the present time. Clairaudience is hearing those things or events, and clairgustance is the peculiar ability to taste food or other objects not in one's mouth. Clairsentience is feeling or sensing something that is happening at another location.

Clairolfaction is a little different from these other types of ESP. In this case, a psychic uses extrasensory smell to interpret spiritual energies—or **auras**—from a person. People with clairolfaction (also called clairalience) say they sense if a person is healthy or if he or she might soon die. This ability can also be used to sense what a person located elsewhere is seeing. For instance, if a person is seeing the ocean, clairolfaction would allow the psychic to smell the salty air of the sea.

Telepathy is sometimes referred to as the ability to "read minds." A telepath receives thoughts or images from another person. Psychometry is similar, but it involves a nonliving object. A psychic can touch an object and receive visions about a person who touched that object at an earlier time.

Telekinesis (also called psychokinesis) is the ability to affect objects without touching them. It is somewhat different from psychometry. It is not about a paranormal version of one of the five senses, but rather it is about making things move or change in some way.

Some people also consider **mediumship**—the ability to contact the dead—a form of ESP because mediums can see and hear beings who exist beyond the normal world.

Some ESP History

People have believed in paranormal powers for thousands of years. Many of these beliefs still survive in tribal cultures in such places as South America, Africa, and Australia. These beliefs, including communications with spirits and animals, as well as the ability of a spiritual leader—sometimes called a shaman—to foresee the future, were followed for a long time. Then religions such as Judaism, Islam, and Christianity began to replace these beliefs.

In the 19th century, especially in England and the United States, a renewed interest in ESP and the paranormal was awakened. A movement called **Spiritualism** became popular in the 1880s in England. Spiritualists were interested in finding out about life after death. They sought to contact the dead through séances and other means. Séances—gatherings of people who want to contact the dead—were led by mediums and often attended by serious scientists and scholars.

The Society for Psychical Research was founded in London, England, in 1882. Three years later, the American Society for Psychical Research was also created. Both organizations were concerned at first with life after death but then they branched out into other areas of study. They researched everything from haunted houses and hypnotism to forms of ESP such as clairvoyance and telekinesis.

Henry Sidgwick, English philosopher and founder of the Society for Psychical Research, c. 1890.

Early Research

These organizations helped spark scientific curiosity in ESP. So did a book written by novelist Upton Sinclair in 1930. His book *Mental Radio* is about experiments he conducted with his wife, Mary. According to Sinclair, Mary could "see" pictures the author drew in another room and then draw copies of them.

Joseph Banks (J.B.) Rhine, a psychologist at Duke University, thought he would try something similar. Rhine has been called the "Father of **Parapsychology**," which is the scientific study of paranormal events. He is often considered the first person to conduct objective tests to see whether telepathy and telekinesis are real.

Rhine created a unique experiment using what he called **Zener cards** to test for telepathy. A deck of Zener cards contains 25 cards. Each card has one of five symbols: a circle, a square, a cross, a star, or three wavy lines. An experimenter sits in one room and

Joseph Banks Rhine used Zener cards to test a person's telepathic abilities.

deals out five of the cards, which can be in any combination. In a completely different room, a person tries to guess which cards were drawn. In an experiment that tested telekinesis, Rhine also tried to see if a person could use his or her mind to control a roll of the dice and make a specific number turn up.

Using these methods, Rhine concluded that in some cases the people being tested guessed correctly or influenced the outcomes on the dice more often than would be possible by chance. In other words, he claimed to have proven that some people have ESP. More recently, however, scientists have said that Rhine's experiments were flawed and so prove nothing.

Why Believe in ESP?

It might be easier to understand that people who do not have access to modern science believe in a phenomenon such as ESP. But in fact many people who live in modern civilizations still believe in it, too. What leads them to think ESP is real?

Disproving ESP

The Committee for the Scientific Investigation of Claims of the Paranormal is a group of scientists who devote themselves to proving that claims of ESP and other such mysteries are not true.

Despite all of our scientific knowledge, there is still a great deal about the world people do not fully understand. For example, animals seem to have abilities that are similar to ESP. When tsunamis smashed into countries such as Thailand, India, and

Kirlian photography shows the aura of living things.

Malaysia in 2004, most the animals in the region had fled to higher ground long before the first huge wave destroyed homes and drowned people. Animals seem to have an extrasensory sense of when disaster is about to hit. And if they have this ability, it seems human beings should have it, too.

Interestingly, aboriginal peoples (native tribes) in Asia were said to also sense disasters. They escaped into the hills with the animals. Could it be that modern people have lost touch with their basic psychic abilities?

There seems to be some physical evidence that people and other living things generate an energy field that some called an aura. In the 1950s, scientists Valentina and Semyon Davidovich Kirlian developed Kirlian photography. This technology allowed them to take pictures of auras. In one remarkable experiment they cut off a piece of a leaf and took a Kirlian photograph of the leaf. The image showed an aura that outlined the entire leaf, including the part that was no longer there. Such evidence makes some people wonder whether ESP is real and whether it is just a matter of time before scientists prove it exists.

Chapter 2

Visions of the Future and the Past

The most common form of ESP is precognition. Sometimes called a **premonition**, this is having a vision or sense of something that is going to happen in the future. There are many stories about premonitions, often helping people avoid disasters. Here is one example told by a woman who was on vacation with her family. It was reported in the book *The Gift* by Sally Rhine Feather (the daughter of J.B. Rhine) and Michael Schmicker:

"My husband and I were on an excursion boat. We had saved and planned for the ride, and the gangplank was already up when I got 'butterflies.' Our two-month-old daughter was with us. I told my husband I was getting off the boat. He thought I was crazy. I said he could stay, but I had to get off, and I asked the men to put the gangplank down."

After they got off, the husband was so mad at his wife he refused to speak to her on the way home. The woman's intuition proved to be precognitive.

"The next news bulletin we heard said that there was a collision, and a freighter had hit the excursion boat we had been on. Within fifteen minutes the excursion boat sunk, though all aboard were rescued."[2]

Web Site Testimonies

Some Web sites invite people who have had precognitive experiences to share them with others. At the *Paranormal Stories Archives*, for instance, a woman related this tale:

One night, I was driving home with a woman friend from a party. We had left our husbands behind because of a late meeting, and I was driving her home. We were on a very dark stretch of a two-lane highway between towns when I suddenly thought there was something wrong about 12 feet ahead of us. There was nothing visible . . . in my headlight. I stopped and my friend asked why was I stopping. I said nothing, but got out of the car and she followed me. Several feet ahead of us in our lane was a very large hole which would have resulted in serious injury, or death, had I driven into it. Someone had removed a wooden "horse" guard and had blown out the pots of flame set out by a highway crew. We had nothing to light the pots with, but did replace the "horse" in front of the hole a few feet ahead of the excavation. We were able to drive around it and proceeded on. My friend called the highway patrol when I dropped her off before proceeding home. I do not know what intuition led me to stop that night.[3]

Dreams

A famous case of precognition occurred in October 1966 in Aberfan, Wales. A ten-year-old girl named Eryl Mai Jones had a dream in which blackness covered her school. On October 21, two days after she told her mother about her dream, a gigantic mudslide washed over the town, including Eryl's school. More than 100 people died, including Eryl.[4]

Other premonitions came before the ill-fated voyage of the *Titanic* in 1912. Some of the passengers said they had dreamed the ship would sink.

Psychiatrist and parapsychologist Ian Stevenson of the University of Virginia . . . researched the cases years later. He discovered about 20 cases of people who had a premonition of the event—many of whose lives were saved as a result. And the Society for Psychical Research still keep[s] the records including an original unused ticket kept by one of those who cancelled.[5]

There have been several documented cases of passengers on the doomed *Titanic* having premonitions that the ocean liner would sink.

Dreams

Famous psychoanalyst Sigmund Freud began studying dreams in the 19th century. Many psychologists today see dreams as keys to understanding the mind, but most do not believe in ESP.

More recently some people claimed that they had dreams about the space shuttle *Challenger* disaster in 1986 and the 9/11 terrorist attacks in 2001 before these tragedies happened. Feather and Schmicker reported several of these in their book *The Gift*, including this one:

> On the night of September 10 [2001], a woman awoke after only an hour or so of sleep after a terrible dream. She was in a large building with many other people when suddenly the whole thing gave way and tumbled into space. Then she was in the dark, crawling among broken pipes and electrical wires. She woke up shaking and crying. Her husband held her until she could breathe. She finally went back to sleep, but shortly woke again with the same dream. This happened a third and fourth time, and only stopped when medication helped her salvage a few hours rest. She had never had such a night before in her life.[6]

Dreams are a very important part of ESP. Back in 1927, a man named J.W. Dune published a book called *On Prophetic Dreams: An Experiment with Time*. In the book he tells how he wrote down all his dreams after he woke up. After doing this many times, he looked back at his notes and found that many of his dreams actually foretold future events.

At Duke University, Louisa E. Rhine, the wife of J.B. Rhine, analyzed over 3,000 cases of precognition and discovered that most of them—68 percent —had occurred during dreams.

Retrocognition and Crime Investigation

Retrocognition—also called postcognition—allows people using ESP to see into the past, to events they did not experience themselves. While it seems that many ordinary people can experience precognitive ESP, retrocognition is more often associated with those who claim to be true psychics.

Law enforcement agencies sometimes enlist the help of psychics such as Annette Martin in their criminal investigations.

Déjà vu

Déjà vu is the strong but brief sensation that a person has experienced or dreamed an event before but is unable to recall specifics of the dream or the earlier event. Some say this may be a form of precognition, but others say it is just a trick of the mind.

There has been a lot of interest in retrocognition and telepathy for investigating crime scenes. When crimes stump detectives, they sometimes turn to psychics for help.

Some psychics claim to have solved crimes, and some of them have become famous. Noreen Renier is one of these. Since the early 1980s she has been involved in over 500 criminal investigations. For example, in a missing person case recorded in the *Houston Chronicle*, Renier said she gave the family of 74-year-old Philip Lester directions so they could find his body after the elderly man disappeared.[7] In addition to postcognition abilities, psychic crime investigators also often use clairvoyance and other ESP powers to learn about events in the present.

Debunkers

Skeptics are people who do not take for granted what, at first, appears to be true. They seek to "debunk" or prove that psychics' claims are just scams. While psychic crime investigators such as Renier appear to have achieved results, skeptics say that they are actually just using tricks to lead people into offering clues.

For example, a family might ask a psychic to help them find a missing uncle. The psychic might close her eyes and say, "I see someone in a uniform. Does this mean something to you?" The family members are shocked because the uncle used to serve in the U.S. Air Force. Actually, this is not so

Skeptics argue that fortune tellers are just really good at reading their clients' body language and do not really have psychic powers.

remarkable at all. The chances are that *someone* in the family wears a uniform of some type, such as that of a nurse, a police officer, a firefighter, or even a maid or a refuse collector.

Another way skeptics say psychics fool people is by looking at body language. A careful observer can tell if a person's breathing quickens, his or her voice changes, or he or she fidgets. Other signals could also tell the psychic that his or her guesses are getting closer to some fact about a crime victim, for example. Fortune tellers—people who use crystal balls and cards to tell paying customers their future —are another example of psychics who are very good at reading people.

Chapter 3

Amazing Senses

While precognition may be the most common form of ESP experienced among ordinary people, the kind that has been most closely examined by scientists is clairvoyance. Clairvoyance, along with related ESP abilities such as clairaudience and clairsentience, allows people to see, hear, or otherwise sense things that are going on in the present moment in a place most other people cannot detect. There are many stories of people sensing other people and events at a distance. People young and old have related such tales as this one:

I have always been able to sense when someone or a family pet has passed. I always seem to know right at the moment it happens. I just

Some people claim to be able to sense events that they cannot possibly see.

somehow know and feel it. My most distinct memory of this ability happened was when I was about 13. I was in school and somehow, I just knew my grandmother on my real father's side had just died. I was living in Connecticut and she was in Texas. Apparently she had been sick for sometime and I was completely unaware of the situation.

When my mother came to pick me up she was about to tell me about my grandmother, when I interrupted her and said Grandma Olivia died. She asked me how I knew. All I could say was I didn't know. Ever since then I can always sense when someone passes, doesn't have to be a family member, just someone I know. I

also have family members that passed fre-
quently visit me in my dreams.[8]

Clairvoyance Research

During the Cold War, when the former Soviet
Union and the United States were struggling with
each other to be the leading world superpower, the
Soviets began a research program to study clairvoyance. It was a very secret program. Nobody in the
United States knew about it until 1970, when the
book *Psychic Discoveries Behind the Iron Curtain*
was published by Sheila Ostrander and Lynn
Schroeder.

The U.S. Central Intelligence Agency (CIA) decided that if the Soviets believed ESP research was
important then America should study it, too. Be-
ginning in 1972 the CIA sponsored psychic research at the Stanford Research Institute (SRI) in
Menlo Park, California.

Several different experiments were performed.
In one, a person whose clairvoyant abilities were
being tested tried to see what kind of object was
placed inside a box. In another, people were shown
a location on a map. They were asked to mentally
travel to that place and describe what they saw. In
still another experiment—more related to telepathy
—one person (a "sender") would try to send a
mental image of an object to a "receiver."

The CIA continued these experiments until
1995, when the federal government decided that

These twin girls are engaged in an experiment to test their clairvoyance. The girl on the left is attempting to draw a picture her sister is looking at behind a screen.

the research was producing no definite results. Also, by this time the Cold War was over and the Soviet Union no longer existed.

Psychic Spies

In the book *Remote Viewers: The Secret History of America's Psychic Spies*, author James Schnabel tells several stories in which psychics hired by the government were supposedly able to spy on people in distant locations. Among the psychics he mentions is Joe McMoneagle.

McMoneagle worked for the CIA, and he was asked on a number of occasions to find out what certain known spies were up to. In a 1980 case he was handed a photo of a man in Europe who was known to be involved in espionage. McMoneagle received a file on the foreign agent and was asked to describe what the man was doing at a particular time.

Using his clairvoyant abilities, McMoneagle told the CIA that he could see the foreign agent driving up a road in some hills. He described what the target agent was wearing, and he described the scene. Suddenly, McMoneagle said he could not see what was happening anymore: "[It is] like I was looking at his picture and the picture turned sideways"[9] and vanished.

Joe McMoneagle was a clairvoyant used by the Pentagon to track foreign spies.

Did McMoneagle fail in his mission? Not exactly. According to Schnabel, the CIA later learned that the foreign agent had accidentally driven his car off a cliff on a hilly road in Italy, where he died.

In another case, McMoneagle helped the CIA discover the solution to a puzzling question: Why were Soviet diplomats and others associated with the Soviet government caught carrying around fishing poles? The Soviets repeatedly asserted they just liked to go fishing a lot. But McMoneagle had a vision of an American man who was working secretly for the Soviets. The man used his fishing pole to retrieve microfilm and other information from a hidden crevice high up on a tower on military property.

Visions of Space

One particularly remarkable case of clairvoyant powers involved a psychic who accurately described a scene that was far off in outer space. The experiment involved the work of SRI researchers Harold E. Puthoff and Russell Targ. The year was 1973, a time

Results in Dispute

Scientists and psychic skeptics David Marks and Robert Kammann refuted Puthoff and Targ's experiments when they were unable to reproduce the same results that Puthoff and Targ reported.

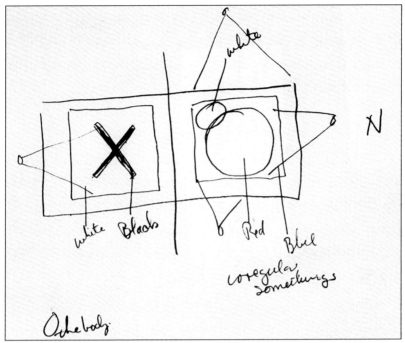

Ingo Swann was the subject of experimentation by the American Society of Psychical Research, testing his clairvoyant power. Ingo Swann drew this picture of figures that were suspended on a platform above his head, which he could not see.

when little was known about the planet Jupiter, except what had been observed using telescopes.

Targ and Puthoff created a challenge for Ingo Swann, a person they were testing for clairvoyant powers. They asked Swann to describe Jupiter in as much detail as possible. Swann began doing so, providing some information that was already known. Then he added a detail that was not known: Jupiter, like Saturn, had rings, although they were much less obvious rings than those on Saturn.

Remarkably, Swann's statement was later confirmed when the NASA space probe *Pioneer 11* reached Jupiter in 1974. Indeed, there were thin rings around the planet.

Other ESP Senses

ESP experiences typically involve sight, or clairvoyance, but some people have reported vivid ESP events involving other senses. These sensations can be just as powerful as having a vision in which something is seen. In *The Gift*, for example, this story was told:

> A high school girl in Ohio was writing a paper for English class when her right arm began to hurt. The pain finally became so bad she couldn't finish the paper and had to stop writing. She couldn't find any reason for the sudden onset of the excruciating pain. That evening, her father was late coming home from work. At 6:30 they [the family] got a phone call. That afternoon, her father's right

---

Human Brain Power

Humans use only 10 percent of their brains for everyday activities. Some people wonder if the other 90 percent might be used for things we do not understand, such as ESP.

---

arm had been caught in the gears of a crane he was operating. The arm had to be amputated.[10]

Any of the five senses can be involved in ESP. However, ESP can also go beyond these senses and into other realms of the mind.

Chapter 4

Mind Reading and Moving Objects

In addition to sensing something that is happening in another place or time, some who say they have the gift of ESP claim to be able to use their minds to read people's thoughts, move objects, or change the outcome of events. Reading the thoughts of others is called telepathy, and moving objects with the mind is called telekinesis.

Magicians or Psychics?

Mind reading and **levitation** (making objects apparently float in the air) are tricks often seen in magic shows. In the 1900s, when Americans and the British were becoming interested in the paranormal, a number of people stepped up to claim special powers.

One of the most famous was Daniel Douglas Home, whose special ability was self-levitation.

The single most famous incident in Home's life occurred in December 1868. At a séance in his London apartment, those in attendance saw his body grow longer. Then he rose from the ground. Upon his descent, he walked into the next room and walked out the window. The attendees saw him apparently floating outside the window, three stories in the air. Home subsequently floated into the room, feet foremost.[11]

It was said that the famous magician Harry Houdini tried to reproduce Home's feat but could never manage it.

Another popular trick was to have an assistant cover the mind reader's eyes with a blindfold. The assistant,

Some people claiming to be mind readers tricked their audiences through the help of an assistant.

Television Trickery

Television and other media make levitation and mind reading easier to perform as **illusions**. There are books and television programs that show audiences exactly how the magicians fool people.

usually a woman, would next ask someone in the audience to tell her something in private, such as a number between one and ten or an object in a purse. The psychic would then guess what it was. What the audience did not know was that, before this show, the psychic—magician, really—had worked out a system to communicate with his assistant in secret.

Some telepaths who have received a great deal of criticism more recently include John Edwards and James Van Praagh. Both have hosted television and radio programs. Van Praagh also is co-executive producer of the series *Ghost Whisperer*. Their critics say they use stage tricks to fool audiences into believing they have ESP abilities.

Telepathy Experiments

While magicians can obviously create some amazing illusions of telepathy and levitation, some scientists believe these ESP abilities could be real.

Famous experiments involving telepathy were conducted in the 1960s and 1970s at the Maimonides

Medical Center in New York City. **Psychiatrist** Montague Ullman and psychologist Stanley Krippner studied whether one person could influence the dreams of another person.

From the early 1960s to the early 1970s, they conducted over 100 tests. In these experiments one person was asleep. Another person looked at a picture and tried to send the image in that picture to the sleeping person's mind so he or she would dream about it. According to Ullman and Krippner, they had some surprising results. The experiments seemed to work in some cases. They published their results in the 1973 book *Dream Telepathy: Experiments in Nocturnal Extrasensory Perception*.

The Ganzfeld Experiment

Other researchers have conducted experiments similar to those performed in Menlo Park, California. For example, at the University of Edinburgh in Scotland, parapsychologist Charles Honorton created a study to prove that people could experience **remote viewing** (clairvoyance). Honorton, like

Parapsychologist Charles Honorton made use of a deprivation chamber, such as the one shown in this picture, in his psychic experiments.

some others who study ESP, believed that clairvoyance and other forms of ESP involved people being able to detect a kind of energy field that was generated by living things and objects. This energy, however, is so weak that it is difficult for most people to detect. Many other sights, sounds, and feelings that surround us interfere with our ability to experience this weak energy.

The solution, Honorton reasoned, was to place people inside a **deprivation chamber**. This could be a room or other enclosed area made soundproof so that outside noise could not get in. Also, the room might be darkened or the person might have his or her eyes covered so they could not see anything. In this way, the subject of the experiment would be open to other sensory input. Honorton called this the "Ganzfeld" experiment. (*Ganzfeld* is a German word that means "whole field.")

As with the CIA experiments at the Stanford Research Institute, Honorton's research involved a "sender" and a "receiver." The sender would view one of four video clips. The receiver, who was in a deprivation chamber, had also seen the four videos but did not know which one the sender would see. Upon watching the video, the sender would use telepathy to tell the receiver which video was the right one.

With four different videos, the chances were one in four (or 25 percent) that the receiver could guess the answer correctly. In the Ganzfeld experiments, though, Honorton recorded a 35 percent (more than one in three) correct response rate. This certainly seemed to show that at least some telepathic action was taking place.

Uri Geller Versus the Amazing Randi

One of the most famous people to practice the art of telekinesis is Uri Geller. Geller became famous in the 1970s for his apparent ability to bend spoons, forks, and other objects with his mind. He could also make the hands on watches slow down, stop, or speed up.

For a long time no one could figure out how Geller was able to bend things. Then James Randi, who as a stage magician called himself the Amazing Randi, showed audiences how silverware can be bent

Uri Geller amazed many with his ability to bend spoons using only his mind, although stage magician James Randi was able to duplicate the feat without using pyschic power.

James Randi is convinced that all forms of ESP are fake. That is why for years he has offered a $1 million prize to anyone who can prove, to his complete satisfaction, that he or she can perform psychic feats. To this day no one has collected the prize money.

using standard magic tricks. Randi continued to perform as a magician for many years. He also has become just as interested in working as a skeptic and debunker of fake psychics.

In 1996 Randi created the James Randi Educational Foundation in Fort Lauderdale, Florida, to educate the public about claims concerning the supernatural and paranormal. It is Randi's concern that too many people can fall for tricks by those who claim to be psychics or to have other supernatural powers. He hopes to prevent any harm happening to ordinary people and to help them become better critical thinkers.

The Pet Psychic

An interesting twist on telepathy is the story of Sonya Fitzpatrick. As a young girl of eleven, Sonya was diagnosed with severe loss of hearing. But the youngster claimed she could hear and talk to various animals on her family farm. She felt that being deaf "honed all my other senses in a way that, I'm convinced, helped me to communicate with animals."[12]

Some thought that Fitzpatrick's deafness worked like a deprivation chamber in a Ganzfeld experiment. She was more open to ESP and, for some reason, connected well with animals. Her connection was broken, however, when the family killed and cooked the geese that she had grown close to.

Pet psychic Sonya Fitzpatrick is known for her ability to communicate with animals.

Her gift of telepathy returned later in life, however, and Fitzpatrick began to share her talent with others. She astounded many and even hosted the television program *The Pet Psychic*. On the show she would help pet owners communicate with their animals, especially animals that were misbehaving in some way or had medical problems that had stumped veterinarians.

Fitzpatrick explains her telepathic bond with animals this way: "Energy in its purest form is the life force of the universe that flows around us and through us. . . . A mind energy link is not broken even though the physical bodies maybe some distance apart."[13]

With so little still known about the human mind, perhaps the connections Fitzpatrick and others make with their minds are, indeed, possible.

Notes

Chapter One: The Sixth Sense

1. Alec Gallup and Frank Newport, *The Gallup Poll: Public Opinion 2005.* New York: Rowman & Littlefield, 2005, p. 221.

Chapter Two: Visions of the Future and the Past

2. Sally Rhine Feather and Michael Schmicker, *The Gift: ESP, the Extraordinary Experiences of Ordinary People.* New York: St. Martin's, 2005, p. 65.

3. Dora K., "Fortunate Precognition," About.com: Paranormal Phenomena. http://paranormal. about.com/library/blstory_april02_35.htm.

4. Jeff Belanger and Kirsten Dalley, *The Nightmare Encyclopedia: Your Darkest Dreams Interpreted.* Career Press, 2005, p. 231.

5. The Psychics and Mediums Network, "Titanic Coincidences." www.psychics.co.uk/coinciden ces/titanic_movie.html.

6. Feather and Michael Schmicker, *The Gift*, p. 170.

7. Stephen Johnson, "Family cites aid of psychic in finding man's remains/Victim, 74, had been

missing since Nov. 30," *Houston Chronicle*, June 8, 1999. http://noreenrenier.com/media/articles/houstonchronicle.htm.

Chapter Three: Amazing Senses

8. Quoted in "I Can Sense When People Die," Psychic Experiences.com. www.psychic-experiences.com/real-psychic-story.php?story=1242.
9. Quoted in James Schnabel, "The CIA Successfully Used Psychic Spies," in *ESP: Fact or Fiction?* Terry O'Neill, ed. Detroit: Greenhaven, 2003, p. 66.
10. Feather and Schmicker, *The Gift*, p. 112.

Chapter Four: Mind Reading and Moving Objects

11. J. Gordon Melton, *The Encyclopedia of Religious Phenomena*. Detroit: Visible Ink, 2008, pp. 153–155.
12. Sonya Fitzpatrick, *Cat Talk: The Secrets of Communicating with Your Cat*. New York: Penguin Group, 2003, p. 2.
13. Fitzpatrick, *Cat Talk*, p. 32.

Glossary

auras: Energy fields that surround all living things that some people say are what makes various kinds of ESP possible.

deprivation chamber: A room or other enclosed space that is kept dark and soundproof, sometimes used so that people can more easily use ESP without interference.

illusions: Things that seems real to the eye but are actually tricks of some kind; things that are not as they appear.

levitation: The act of lifting objects or people into the air using magic or telekinesis.

mediumship: The practice of using ESP to make contact with dead people.

paranormal: Anything that is beyond normal human experience that cannot be easily measured, described, or tested using science.

parapsychology: The scientific study of the paranormal.

premonition: Another word for precognition; an unexplained feeling that something is going to happen before it does.

psychiatrist: A medical doctor who specializes in studying how the human mind works.

psychics: People with ESP abilities.

psychologists: Scientists who study how the human mind works and how to treat those with mental or emotional illnesses. Unlike psychiatrists, psychologists do not need a medical degree to practice.

remote viewing: A phrase that means the same as clairvoyance; seeing things at a distance that are beyond the normal field of vision.

skeptics: People who doubt claims about the paranormal and want them to be proven, beyond reasonable doubt, through scientific methods.

Spiritualism: A 19th century religious movement that focused mainly on proving the existence of life after death.

Zener cards: A deck of 25 cards—five sets, each set having one of five symbols—that is used to test clairvoyance and telepathy in scientific experiments.

For Further Exploration

Books

Michael Martin, *ESP: Extrasensory Perception*, Mankato, MN: Capstone, 2006. A short overview of ESP, including history of and research on psychic phenomena.

Chris Oxlade, *The Mystery of ESP*, Chicago: Reed Educational & Professional Publishing, 2002. Explains what ESP is believed to be and focuses on what science has done to try to prove whether or not it exists.

Web Sites

Extrasensory Perceptions Guide (www.extrasensory-perceptions-guide.com/extrasensory-perception.html). This Web site has definitions of different types of ESP phenomena, as well as discussions about dreams, angels, herbal remedies, and other areas related to spiritual issues.

The Mystica (www.themystica.com/mystica/articles/e/esp_extrasensory_perception.html). An online encyclopedia of the paranormal, this site offers a history and explanation of ESP as well as firsthand stories from people who have experienced ESP.

The Skeptic's Dictionary (www.skepdic.com/esp.html). A Web site that offers a skeptics view of ESP.

Index

Picture Credits

About the Author

Kevin Hile is a freelance writer, editor, and Web site designer based in Michigan. A graduate of Adrian College, where he met his wife, Janet, he has been a reference book editor for 20 years. Hile is a former Detroit Zoo volunteer who is currently a docent and Web site manager for the Potter Park Zoo in Lansing. Deeply concerned about the environment, animals, and wildlife conservation, he is also the author of *Animal Rights* (Chelsea House, 2004) and *Little Zoo by the Red Cedar* (2008). Hile is a regular contributor to Gale's Contemporary Authors series. He is also the author of *Dams and Levees*, *Ghost Ships*, and *Centaurs* for KidHaven Press.